I have placed emphasis on some selected Scripture by the use of bold print.

If you find this booklet helpful, please go to ***thirdgreatestcommandment.org***, download a free digital copy, and help me distribute it as far and wide as possible by email or other social media, attaching the booklet or referring them to the above website. Also, you may order hard copies of this booklet through the above website or through Amazon.

My email address is jerry@thirdgreatestcommandment.org.

ISBN: 979-8-9995947-8-5

One of the most important aspects of the Christian life is learning to walk closely with Jesus every day. In *Third Greatest Commandment?*, Jerry Murray reminds us that abiding in Christ is essential if we are going to experience the power of the Holy Spirit, grow in obedience, and faithfully share the Gospel with others. My prayer is that this booklet will encourage believers to deepen their daily walk with Christ and live on mission for the sake of the Great Commission.

Kevin Ezell
President
North American Mission Board, SBC

CONTENTS

PREFACE

A Jewish scribe once asked Jesus, "Which is the first commandment of all?" And Jesus answered him, "The first of all the commandments is: 'Hear, O Israel, the Lord our God, the Lord is one. And you shall love the Lord your God with all your heart, with all your soul, with all your mind, and with all your strength. This is the first commandment. And the second, like it, is this: You shall love your neighbor as yourself.' There is no other commandment greater than these." (Mk. 12:28-31) These two commandments are the greatest because of the ultimate power of love as demonstrated by Jesus on the cross and as expressed in 1 Cor. 13:13, which says, "but the greatest of these is love." Also, if we obey these two great commandments, we will automatically obey all others. But how do we obey these two great commandments? The only way we can obey these two is to follow God's command to **abide in Christ!** (Jn. 15:4) "...For without Me, You can do nothing." (Jn.15:5) Jesus never identified a **third greatest commandment**, but if He had, what would it be? I believe it would be to **"abide in Him"**. As we **abide in Christ**, we engage the power of the Holy Spirit to help us obey all of God's commandments and achieve so much more. Brother Lawrence said, "If I were a preacher, I would preach nothing **but practicing the presence of God**.", which is to **abide in Christ**. And C.S. Lewis said,"**Abiding in Christ** is the essence of the promise of the New Covenant."

The commandment, **"Abide in Me"**, is so important that most of John Chapter 15 and most of the entire book of First John is dedicated to it. Also, this commandment is reflected throughout the Bible in many other ways: **dwell in Your presence; walk in the Spirit; walk in the Light; acknowledge Him in all your ways; fix your eyes on Jesus; whose mind is stayed on You; meditate in it day and night; on You I wait all the day; praise continually; pray without ceasing; seek God's face; remain in Him; hold fast to Him; live with Him; live through Him; and be filled with the Spirit**. The last term, **"be filled with the Spirit"**, has been the subject of much confusion over the years, but the meaning is quite simple. Ephesians 5:18 says, "And do not be drunk with wine, in which is dissipation, but **be filled with the Spirit**." In other words, don't be under the influence of wine or other worldly things, but be **under the constant influence of the Holy Spirit**, who abides in all Christians from the time of salvation, and who wants all Christians to **abide in Him**.

Jesus said, "I have come that they may have life, and that they may have it more abundantly." (Jn. 10:10) But how could that abundant life be so worthwhile when most Christians appear on the surface to be no better off than non-Christians? This little booklet, which is for both Christians and non-Christians alike, explains how both could be true. It also explains the **key** to attaining the full extent of the more abundant life, which is to **abide in Christ all the time**. Charles Stanley emphasized that "**abiding in Christ** is crucial for a fulfilling Christian life, involving dwelling, remaining, and staying in a relationship with Him. He believed that abiding in Christ provides rest for the soul, fruitful service, answered prayer, and confidence in God's love. **Abiding in Christ** is not just a passive state but requires daily practice of **walking in dependence on the Holy Spirit and in submission to God's Word**."

Have you ever wondered what that **"more abundant life"** here on earth should look like? Just one of the many aspects of a **"more abundant life"** is **victory over sin**, and one of the many benefits of **abiding in Christ is victory over sin**. As you can imagine, that can be a big deal! I am not saying that you can become perfect, but you can be successful in minimizing sin in your life.

Romans 7:19 reminds us that, "For the good that I will to do, I do not do; but the evil I will not to do, that I practice." And Romans 7:24-25 goes on to say, "O wretched man that I am! Who will deliver me from this body of death? I thank God - **through Jesus Christ our Lord!**" We are commanded to **live our lives through Jesus Christ by abiding in Him**. First Corinthians 10:13 says, "No temptation has overtaken you except such as is common to man; but God is faithful, who will not allow you to be tempted beyond what you are able, but with the temptation will also make **the way of escape**..." And in John 14:6, Jesus said, "**I am the way**..." So, if you **follow Jesus with your thoughts throughout the day**, engaging the power of the Holy Spirit (**abiding in Him**), you will have victory over sin! The Apostle John confirms this in First John 3:6, where he wrote,"**Whoever abides in Him does not sin...**" And Galations 5:16 says, **"I say then: 'Walk in the Spirit and you shall not fulfill the lust of the flesh.'"** You have probably already concluded that just trying harder on your own to avoid sin does not work. "...For without me, you can do nothing." (Jn. 15:5) "There is therefore now no condemnation to those who are in Christ Jesus, who do not walk according to the flesh, but **according to the Spirit**. For the **law of the Spirit of life in Christ Jesus** has made me free from the law of sin and death." (Ro. 8:1-2) Also, Jesus demonstrated **the way** to successfully avoid sin in Luke Chapter 4 as He was **"filled with the Spirit"**. He also focused on and quoted pertinent Scripture verses, which is one of the many ways to **abide in Him**.

Another one of the many benefits of **abiding in Christ is boldness for sharing Jesus** with lost people. "...They were all **filled with the Holy Spirit, and they spoke the word of God with boldness**." (Acts 4:31) Most Christians do not share Jesus with others because they are not **abiding in Him**, "for without Me, you can do nothing." (Jn. 15:5) The more disciplined you become **practicing His presence**, the more victory you will have over sin in your life, the more passion and boldness you will have for sharing Jesus and the more you will enjoy the many other benefits of the **"more abundant life."**

Although the subject of **abiding in Christ** can be found throughout the Bible, it seems that most Christians, including myself, have overlooked its significance in attaining the full extent of the **"more abundant life."** Regrettably, it took me about fifty years, as a Christian, before I identified, studied, and embraced the many Scripture verses on this subject, even though I had served as an elder, deacon, small-group leader and Sunday School teacher!

During the summer of 2016, my wife, Rhoda, and I visited The Cove in western North Carolina where we heard a great presentation on the power of the Holy Spirit.

The speaker was Pastor Jonathan Falwell from Thomas Road Baptist Church (TRBC) in Lynchburg, Virginia. His talk peaked my interest, and I was reminded that the power of the Holy Spirit is one of the most important subjects in the Bible. I pursued that interest by reading several books on the Holy Spirit and on **abiding in Christ**. While reading the Bible during the following years, I was drawn to many related Scripture verses that seemed to jump from the pages. That focus helped me understand more fully, and I finally began trying to develop the discipline of **abiding in Christ** in my own life. Eventually, I felt compelled to share what I had learned by writing this booklet based on a multitude of notes that I had collected over the years.

Abiding in Christ is so important because it engages the power of the Holy Spirit in our lives. And "His divine power has given to us all things that pertain to life and godliness...". (2 Pet. 1:3) HIs power helps Christians mature spiritually, make a meaningful impact for God's Kingdom, and fulfill God's main purpose for our lives, which is to glorify Him. Also, I am convinced that the best chance for a spiritual revival to occur, both for an individual and for the church body, is through Christians engaging the power of the Holy Spirit by **abiding in Christ continually**. Second Chronicles 7:14 says, "If my people who are called by My name will humble themselves, **and pray and seek My face**, and turn from their wicked ways, then I will hear from heaven, and will forgive their sin and heal their land." To **"pray without ceasing"** (1 Thess. 5:17) and to **"seek God's face"** is to **abide in Him all the time**. And **abiding in Him** is what equips us to turn from our wicked ways, which leads to healing.

There are many excellent books on the subject of **abiding in Christ**. So, you might ask, "Why write another book? In addition to the great emphasis on the importance of **abiding in Christ** as the **third greatest commandment**, this booklet identifies sixteen biblical terms that mean the same thing as abiding, fifteen practical ways of abiding and fifteen Bible-based benefits of abiding, to include **the way** to victory over sin, **the way** to boldness for witnessing and a very important way to help start a revival. It also includes a detailed Gospel message along with the best way to jump-start the Christian journey of new-born Christians. Furthermore, I'm sure you will enjoy and benefit from reading the many enlightening and profound quotes, on this subject, from twenty-two of the greatest Christian authors of all times: Moses, King David, Luke, Apostle John, Apostle Paul, Andrew Murray, A.W. Tozer, Bill Bright, Billy Graham, Brother Lawrence, Charles Spurgeon, Charles Stanley, C.S. Lewis, D.L. Moody, Elmer Towns, Herbert Lockyer, John Piper, R.A. Torrey, Ruth Paxson, Sarah Young, Warren Wiersbe, and Watchman Nee.

Finally, this booklet is much more than just a read-it-once and throw-it-away document. It offers the ability to download a free digital copy from **thirdgreatestcommandment.org**,which provides an easy and efficient way to spread the Gospel and the vital truth about abiding in Christ all the time. This booklet explains the essence of the New Testament: The Gospel of Jesus Christ, how to receive Him as Lord and Savior and how to walk extremely close with Him all day long as you **abide in Him**.

INTRODUCTION

Early one morning about four-thousand years ago, the Jewish patriarch, Jacob, awoke and said, "Surely the Lord is in this place, and I did not know it." (Gen. 28:16) Can you imagine? Of all people, Jacob, the father of the twelve tribes of Israel, was not aware of God's presence! Christians today experience that same extremely significant problem, and it appears that most Christians don't even realize they have that problem! The failure of Christians to maintain an **awareness of God's presence and abide in Him continually**, is one of our greatest problems because we miss out on experiencing many of the benefits the Holy Spirit has for us! Herbert Lockyer, minister and best-selling author of over fifty Christian books back in the 20th Century, once said, "Banks have what are called unclaimed deposits. Often these were owned by people who lived and died in poverty. Can it be that we have a vast unclaimed deposit in God's treasury? Do we live in spiritual penury, a hand to mouth existence, and yet have such wealth at our disposal?"

Before pursuing further the fascinating subject of **abiding in God's presence** today, it is important to review some relevant biblical background. Christians already understand the basics of what I am about to cover, but I think most of you will learn important details about the mystery of Christ and how those details relate to **abiding in Him** and to the **"more abundant life"** that Jesus promised.

God created the first man, Adam, with a free will to live either in obedience to God and **remain in His presence**, or to live according to his desire for a self-centered and sinful life away from God, who gave Adam just one command: "But of the tree of the knowledge of good and evil you shall not eat, for in the day that you eat of it you shall surely die." (Gen. 2:17) Adam rejected God through his sin. "...She also gave to her husband with her, and he ate." (Gen. 3:6) Adam knew that he had done wrong and tried to hide from **God's presence**. "And they heard the sound of the Lord God walking in the garden in the cool of the day, and Adam and his wife hid themselves from the **presence of the Lord God** among the trees of the garden." (Gen. 3:8) God then sent him out from **His presence** in the Garden of Eden. "Therefore the Lord God sent him out of the Garden of Eden to till the ground from which he was taken." (Gen. 3:23) On that day, Adam died spiritually in his relationship with God, rejecting **God's precious presence**, and he later died physically.

So, as our first ancestor, Adam chose a sinful nature that we all inherited from him. "For as by one man's disobedience many were made sinners..." (Ro. 5:19) "For all have sinned and fall short of the glory of God." (Ro. 3:23) Unfortunately, the penalty for sin is eternal separation from **God's presence** and death in Hell. "For the wages of sin is death..." (Rom. 6:23) However, God loves all of us so much that He provided **a way** to forgive our sins and offer us eternal life in **His presence**. Jesus said to him, '**I am the way**, the truth, and the life. No one comes to the Father except through Me.'" (Jn. 14:6)

"Christ died for our sins according to the Scriptures, and that He was buried, and that He rose again the third day according to the Scriptures..." (1Cor. 15:3-4) "For Christ also suffered once for sins, the just for the unjust, that He might **bring us to God**..." (1 Pet. 3:18) "For God so loved the world that He gave His only begotten Son, that whoever **believes in Him** should not perish but have everlasting life." (Jn. 3:16)

The common understanding of the word believe today is simply to accept the facts about something as being true. However, the Greek word for believe, pisteuo, which is used in the New Testament, means not only to believe the facts about Jesus; but to trust Him with all your heart; repent from your sins and from rejecting Jesus; call on Him; receive Him as Lord and Savior; and commit to following Him for the rest of your life. These are not good works, but simply an explanation of the term, believe in Jesus. The term "faith plus nothing" is still valid. Without an understanding of the Greek word pisteuo, when hearing that one must believe in Jesus, the English word believe in today's Bible, can be misunderstood as just accepting the facts about Jesus to be true. The word believe, therefore, falls short in translating the full and accurate meaning of pisteuo. James 2:19 says, "You believe that there is one God. You do well. Even the demons believe - and tremble!" Just believing the facts about Jesus was not good enough to save the demons, nor is it good enough to save us. So, without a proper explanation of pisteuo, a statement that, "All you have to do is believe," can be misleading, and can result in a false sense of salvation, or at best, encourage lukewarm

Christianity. Also, it provides a poor example of how to present the Gospel to a non-Christian.

Many years ago, the world-famous evangelist, Billy Graham, received a letter that said, "I've heard people say that all I have to do to get to heaven is to believe in Jesus. Well, I think I believe in Jesus, but down inside I'm not at all sure I'll go to heaven when I die. In fact, I kind of doubt if I will. What am I missing?" Billy responded by saying, "I'm thankful you've taken the time to write and ask this question - because the most important decision you will ever make is where you will spend eternity. The Bible warns, 'How shall we escape if we ignore such a great salvation?' (Heb. 2:3) What you've heard is right: All we have to do to get into heaven is to believe in Jesus. Jesus Himself said, 'Whoever believes in the Son has eternal life.' (Jn. 3:36) But what does it mean to believe in Jesus? Does that mean simply to believe that he existed, or even that He came down from heaven to save us? No, to believe in Jesus means far more than this. It means first of all that we understand who He is: the only Son of God, sent from heaven to save us from our sins. It means we also understand what He did for us: He died on the cross to take away our sins. The Bible says, 'This is love: not that we loved God, but that he loved us and sent His Son as an atoning sacrifice for our sins.' (1 Jn. 4:10) But to believe in Jesus also means to trust Him as our Savior, and commit our lives to Him as our Lord. In other words, to believe in Jesus is to turn our lives over to Him completely and without reserve. And this is what I urge you to do. By a simple prayer of faith commit your life to Jesus Christ today."

The word **pisteuo** has a special place in my heart even beyond the rich biblical meaning. Early one morning a few years ago, I was preparing to teach an evangelism class. I wanted to explain the critical Greek word, **pisteuo**, but I don't know the Greek language; so I had to depend on what I could find through research. I was thinking that it would be nice to be a Greek scholar to have more confidence in what I was teaching. Later that morning, my wife and I went to the local hospital as volunteers. Our job was to visit about thirty patients each in separate departments. When I visited my last patient, I discovered that **he was a Greek scholar with reference books and all!** He was also a very gifted artist. We had a wonderful conversation about the word **pisteuo** and he confirmed my understanding. We were interrupted by his nurse, and I left his room so overwhelmed by my experience that I forgot to get his name. As I now look back on that special day, I can't help from wondering if he was an angel, who God placed in my path.

There are many great verses in the Bible that refer to **believing in Jesus**, and they provide more in-depth insight into the meaning of this term. Most of them use at least one of these seven key words: **believe, trust, repent, call, confess, receive and follow**. Here are seven of these verses:

> "**...Believe on the Lord Jesus Christ**, and you will be saved..." (Acts:16:31)
>
> "O You who save those who **trust** in You." (Ps. 17:7)

“**Repent**, and let every one of you be baptized in the name of Jesus Christ for the remission of sins, and you shall receive the gift of the Holy Spirit.” (Acts 2:38)

“For whoever **calls on the name of the Lord** shall be saved.” (Ro. 10:13)

“That if you **confess with your mouth the Lord Jesus and believe in your heart** that God has raised Him from the dead, you will be saved.” (Ro. 10:9)

“But as many as **received Him**, to them He gave the right to become children of God, to those who **believe in His name**.” (Jn. 1:12)

“My sheep hear My voice, and I know them, and **they follow Me**. And I give them eternal life…” (Jn. 10:27-28)

These verses should not be looked at as a checklist of actions to take for salvation, because they all basically mean the same thing: **embrace God’s word as expressed in these verses, and embrace Jesus as Lord and Savior**. Salvation will then come in a flash. You will then become a forgiven, born-again child of God, and you can look forward to **abiding in Jesus now and spending eternity in the presence of the Lord** along with all other born-again believers. The only alternative is to experience “everlasting destruction from the **presence of the Lord** and from the glory of His power…” (2 Thess. 1:9) “And anyone not found written in the Book of Life was cast into the lake of fire." (Rev. 20:15). The choice is yours to make!

I have asked many people over the years if they knew for sure they would have eternal life in Heaven when they die, and most of them answered, "I hope so." Well, "I hope so" is not good enough because it is possible and very important to know for sure. First John 5:13 says, "These things I have written to you who believe in the name of the Son of God, that you may know that you have eternal life..." And in the previous verses 11 and 12, it says, "And this is the testimony: that God has given us eternal life, and this life is in His Son. He who has the Son has life, he who does not have the Son of God does not have life." And Second Corinthians 13:5 says, "Examine yourselves as to whether you are in the faith. Test yourselves. Do you not know yourself, that Jesus Christ is in you? - unless indeed you are disqualified." Have you repented, invited Jesus, the Son of God, into your life, trusting Him as your Lord and Savior? "Therefore, if anyone is in Christ, he is a new creation, old things have passed away; behold, all things have become new." (2 Cor. 5:17) If you are born again, there will be good changes in your life. "You will know them by their fruits." (Mt. 7:16). Are you following Jesus with your life? Do you know for sure?

Your commitment to **follow Jesus** includes serving Him as He directs your life. "...Those who have **believed in God** should be careful to maintain good works." (Ti. 3:8) However, God saves us by His grace through faith, not by our good works. The good works help express our love and appreciation for all He has done and will do for us. "For by grace you have been saved through faith, and that not of yourselves, it is the gift of God, not of works, lest anyone should boast. For we are His workmanship, created in Christ Jesus for good works, which God prepared beforehand that we should walk in them." So, your purpose and mission in life, as a Christian, is to glorify God by serving Him with your spiritual gift(s) and other abilities.

Our faith **in Him** and His sacrifice of His very special blood provides the power to forgive all of our sins. "Knowing that you were not redeemed with corruptible things, like silver or gold, from your aimless conduct received by tradition from your fathers, but with the precious blood of Christ, as of a lamb without blemish and without spot." (1 Pet. 1:18-19)

Watchmen Nee, author of The Normal Christian Life said, "Do you believe the Lord would cleanse away all our sins and then leave us to get rid of the sin-producing factory? He was, of course, referring to our sin nature **in Adam**, which produces sin in us. Thankfully, like our faith **in Jesus** and the cleansing power of His blood provides forgiveness of our sins, so our faith **in Jesus** and His death on the cross, burial and resurrection provides the power and means for us to die spiritually to our inherited sinful nature **in Adam**, and to be born again spiritually **in Christ** for newness of life. "Therefore, if anyone is **in Christ**, he is a new creation; old things have passed away; behold, all things have become new." (2 Cor. 5:17) "...so also by one Man's obedience many will be made righteous." (Ro. 5:19)

It is very important to have a basic understanding of the terms **in Adam** and **in Christ**. We were all **in Adam** because he was our first ancestor, and our physical bodies came from him. If he had never lived, we would never have been born. Unfortunately, we inherited his sinful nature, and we were also **in Adam** in that way. Christians were **in Christ** in a spiritual way because we came from Him spiritually when we were born again. "But as many as received Him, to them He gave the right to become children of God, to those who **believe in His name**." (Jn. 1:12) If Christ had never been born, we could never have been born again spiritually. "Just as He chose us in Him before the foundation of the world, that we should be holy and without blame before Him in love." (Eph. 1:4) "In Him also we have obtained an inheritance..." (Eph. 1:11) As born-again Christians, we inherited His spiritual nature in the person of the Holy Spirit. "...You were sealed with the Holy Spirit of promise, who is the guarantee of our inheritance..." (Eph. 1:13-14) We were therefore delivered from that old sinful nature **in Adam**. "...our old man was crucified **with Him**, that the body of sin might be done away with, that we should no longer be slaves of sin." (Ro. 6:6) We can now **abide in Him** as **the way** of doing away with sin because He is **in us** as Christians. The song, **In Christ Alone**, expresses it well with the words, **"I am His and He is mine"**.

Our union **in Christ** makes the biggest difference in the world. "For if we have been united together in the likeness of His death, certainly we also shall be in the likeness of His resurrection..." (Ro. 6:5) So, since we were **in Christ** when He experienced death and then victory through His resurrection, we also can have victory over sin and death. "Therefore, if anyone is **in Christ**, he is a new creation; old things have passed away; behold all things have become new." (2 Cor. 5:17)

Jesus said, "And I will pray the Father, and He will give you another Helper, that He may abide with you forever." (Jn. 14:16) "Do you not know that your body is the temple of the Holy Spirit who is **in you**, whom you have from God, and you are not your own? For you were bought at a price..." (1 Cor. 6:19-20) And "...He who is in you is greater than he who is in the world." (1 Jn. 4:4) So, now we can see the perfect union between God and His people! We are **in Christ** and He is **in us!** "...He who abides **in Me**, and I **in Him**, bears much fruit: for without Me you can do nothing." (Jn. 15:5) The bearing of that fruit relates back to the **"more abundant life"** that Jesus offers and to the key to attaining it. So, let's continue with our focus now on **abiding in the presence of God** today as Adam should have done ages ago.

WHAT DOES IT MEAN TO ABIDE IN CHRIST?

The Holy Spirit abides or dwells in all Christians from the time of salvation and He wants all Christians to **abide in Him.** Dr. Elmer L. Towns, co-founder of Liberty University and author of more than a hundred Christian books, said **"Abiding in Christ is a continuous vital connection to Jesus, characterized by reliance, obedience, prayer, and engagement with God's Word, resulting in fruitfulness, joy, and spiritual empowerment."** It is not just a matter of occasionally checking in with God each day and then going back to life as usual. **Abiding in Him** is about the daily Christian life as God intended it to be. It requires a concerted effort to develop a habit of **remaining focused on Christ** no matter what is going on in your life. As you **abide in Him**, He will help you be who He wants you to be and do what He wants you to do.

The Apostle Paul said, "I have been crucified with Christ; it is no longer I who live, but Christ lives in me; and the life which I now life in the flesh I live by faith in the Son of God, who loved me and gave Himself for me." (Gal. 2:20) The personal evidence of Christ living in you appears as your mind **dwells in His presence**. "For those who live according to the flesh set their minds on the things of the flesh, but those who **live according to the Spirit, the things of the Spirit**. For to be carnally minded is death, but to be **spiritually minded** is life and peace." (Ro. 8:5-6) "I say then: 'Walk in the Spirit and you shall not fulfill the lust of the flesh." (Gal. 5:16) When we walk in the

Spirit as Jesus walked, we take our steps in life **abiding or dwelling mentally in God's presence**.

When we first become spiritually "born again", we are mere babies in Christ. Apostle Paul explained this point in First Corinthians 3:1-3, "And I, brethren, could not speak to you as to spiritual people but as to carnal, as to babes in Christ. I fed you with milk and not with solid food; for until now you were not able to receive it, and even now you are still not able; for you are still carnal. For where there are envy, strife, and divisions among you, are you not carnal and behaving like mere men?" Spiritual growth and Christian maturity normally advance slowly when we are only occasionally **filled and influenced by the Holy Spirit**. But when we are **constantly influenced by the Spirit** through His **ongoing filling**, the maturity process can be much faster and much more fruitful, just like the growth of a farmer's crops can be much faster by being planted in rich soil and having the right amount of sunshine, rain, and fertilizer. Based on my observations, it seems that most Christians spend a lifetime without **remaining filled and influenced by the Spirit** and, therefore, remain "infants in Christ." This explains why most Christians normally act little different than non-Christians.

Bible teacher, missionary and author, Ruth Paxson, provided more insight: "Many people have been baptized with the Holy Spirit into the body of Christ, and they are going to heaven. But they are missing so much of what God wants them to have in this life. Consciously or unconsciously they are more interested in imitating the world system dominated by Satan than in imitating Christ.

Their gifts are often unused, and spiritual fruit is absent from their lives. Nor do they have any great concern to evangelize the spiritually needy in their own community. Their zeal to walk in obedience to the commandments of Christ grows weak. Their devotional life is uneven, if not totally neglected, and they anticipate reading the news more than reading the Word of God. If they do pray, it is a cheerless duty and a tedious task rather than a joy. As with Lot in Sodom, sin for them has lost some of its sinfulness; their sensitivity to sin has been numbed and the edge of conscience blunted. Known sins remain unconfessed. Christians so often lack the **fullness of the Spirit** with its true dependence on God's power for their ministry."

There is a considerable amount of more evidence that further leads me to believe that most Christians today are not constantly filled and influenced by the Holy Spirit:

- 50% rate of Christian divorces
- Living together outside of marriage
- Millions of abortions
- Declining Christian influence on other social mores
- Closing churches

No wonder Christianity has such a bad reputation with many non-Christians and is the object of ridicule and even hatred. Unfortunately, during the past two thousand years, the unveiling of God's mystery through Apostle Paul has been gradually obscured by Satan and by the clouds of time. No way does Satan want us to thoroughly understand and **practice the presence** of God because the Holy Spirit is the source of power for a dynamic and successful Christian life.

Herbert Lockyer reflected on this sad state of Christianity when he said, "Although we have more volumes than ever before expounding the graces and gifts of the Spirit, we fear that such enlightenment is sadly neglected by the vast majority of Christians." He also emphasized that, "The secret of constant personal victory over all that is alien to His holy will is the **abiding consciousness of the holiness of Him** before whom the seraphim veil their faces."

Billy Graham emphasized that, "The ideal Christian life comes as we are **filled with the Holy Spirit** - as He works in and through us as we are yielded to God and His will." He further explained that, "The **Spirit-filled life** is intended for all, needed by all, and available to all."

Most evangelical church leaders encourage their people to glorify God by treating everyone in loving ways with Christ-like characteristics, to be active in serving God and others, and to share their faith with non-Christians. The only way that Christians can be most effective in doing so is to **constantly abide in Christ**: "for without Me, you can do nothing." (Jn. 15:5) Herbert Lockyer explained, "If churches today were **controlled by the Holy Spirit** as in apostolic days, their lives and work would be entirely revolutionized!"

Many of the early Christians were so strongly **filled, influenced, and empowered by the Holy Spirit** that they were willing to give their lives as martyrs while beginning a movement that spread the Gospel of Jesus Christ around the world! In addition to seeing a multitude of lost people come to Christ, they also experienced many other God-given benefits while they were **filled with the Holy Spirit**. Christians today have the potential of living such a **Spirit-filled life**. God wants His stream of living water to continuously flow throughout every day and throughout every hour so it can overflow to others for a fruit-producing, God-glorifying, abundant life. Herbert Lockyer put it this way: "If, then, we **live in His company and maintain a personal, unbroken relationship with Him,** we shall become like Him in purpose, desires, thoughts, spiritual ideals and ambitions."

There are many good reasons why we should **abide in Christ**. The most important reason is that He commands us to do so. Bill Bright, founder of Campus Crusade for Christ said: "This command of God means to **be constantly and continually filled, controlled and empowered with the Holy Spirit as a way of life**. This amazing fact that Christ lives in you and expresses His love through you is one of the most important truths in the word of God... Now, through His indwelling presence, He wants to enable all who place their trust in Him to live this same supernatural life." He not only wants us to live this kind of life, but He commands it." Here are several examples of those commands:

> "**Abide in Me**, and I in you. As the branch cannot bear fruit of itself, unless it abides in the vine, neither can you, unless you abide in Me." (Jn. 15:4)

"And do not be drunk with wine, in which is dissipation; but **be filled with the Spirit**." (Eph. 5:18)

"I say then: **Walk in the Spirit**, and you shall not fulfill the lust of the flesh." (Gal. 5:16)

"Rejoice always, **pray without ceasing, in everything give thanks**; for this is the will of God in Christ Jesus for you." (1 Thess. 5:16-17)

"From the rising of the sun to the place where it sets, the name of the Lord is to be praised." (Ps. 113:3)

The presence of the Holy Spirit, as expressed in the Old Testament, was somewhat different than expressed in the New Testament. With a few exceptions, in the Old Testament, His presence was with His children instead of in His children. "Have I not commanded you? Be strong and of good courage; do not be afraid, nor be dismayed, for the Lord your God is **with you** wherever you go." (Josh. 1:9) However, God sent the Holy Spirit to abide within every Christian after Jesus was glorified through His resurrection. What a wonderful gift!

MORE QUOTES FROM FAMOUS AUTHORS

I would like to share with you many other helpful, thought-provoking, and profound quotes from several well-known and respected Christian authors of the past, that help explain the concept of **abiding in Christ**:

In his book, The Secret of the **Abiding Presence**, Andrew Murray explained:

- "Everything depends **on the ongoing awareness of the Holy Spirit's presence, and the ceaseless communications with Him." "I must spend all of my time with God!**"

- "The measure of the power of the Spirit in us will be the measure of our **experience of the presence of Christ**."

- "Obedience depends on God's presence and power, and it is obedience that helps insure **ongoing filling and remaining in Christ**."

- "As I experience the **constant awareness of God's presence** and related benefits, I will be confident as I share these truths with others."

- When Paul said, "...Christ lives in me." (Gal. 2:20), "he spoke of an actual, divine, unceasing abiding of Christ in him, working in him from hour to hour all that was pleasing to the Father. Only as far as I can **live Christ before their eyes** can I help them understand the complete Gospel message."

In his book, How to Pray, R.A. Torrey wrote:

- "To **abide in Christ**...is to renounce all life independent of Christ, and **constantly to look to Him** for the inflow of His life into us, and the outworking of His life through us. When we do this, and in so far as we do this, our prayers will obtain that which we seek from God."

Here are quotes from The Practice of the Presence of God, by Brother Lawrence (Nicolas Herman):

- **"It is not Your gifts that I seek and desire, but Yourself**, and I can be content with nothing less."The most holy and necessary **practice in our spiritual life is practicing the presence of God**." He also insisted, **"If I were a preacher, I would preach nothing but practicing the presence of God."**

- "I don't know what God has in store for me, but I feel so serene that it doesn't matter. What do I have to be afraid of when I'm **with Him**? By **dwelling in the presence of God**, he has established such a sweet communion with the Lord that his **spirit abides**, without much effort, in the restful peace of God. In this center of rest, he is filled with a faith that equips him to handle anything that comes into his life."

- Brother Lawrence insisted that, "To be **constantly aware of God's presence (and**

filled), it is necessary to form the **habit of continually talking with Him** throughout each day. To think that we must abandon conversation with Him in order to deal with the world is erroneous." He further stated, "During my work, I would always **continue to speak to the Lord** as though He was right with me, offering Him my services and thanking Him for His assistance." Brother Lawrence "believed it was a serious mistake to think of our prayer time as being different from any other. He said his prayers consisted totally and simply of God's presence." He "described the **presence of God or the fullness of His Spirit** as a quiet, familiar conversation with God."

- "Finally, although this exercise may be difficult at first to maintain, it has marvelous effects on the soul when it is faithfully practiced. It draws the graces of the Lord down in abundance and shows the soul how to **see God's presence** everywhere with a pure and loving vision, which is the holiest, firmest, easiest, and the most effective attitude for prayer."

John Piper emphasized that:

- "**Abiding in Christ**, as depicted in John 15, means **hour-by-hour trusting in Jesus** to meet all needs and be all treasure, **staying connected to the vine (Christ)** for life-giving nourishment, and bearing fruit through that connection."

A.W. Tozer emphasized that:

- "**Abiding in Christ is a continuous act of living in union with Jesus**, rather than a passive state. He stressed that it's not an automatic process, but a deliberate choice to remain in the union."

Charles Spurgeon emphasized that:

- **Abiding in Christ is essential for bearing fruit and experiencing God's power**, comparing it to a branch remaining connected to the vine. He believed that fellowship with Christ is a cure for every ill and that **abiding in Him leads to a life of joy and victory**."

HOW CAN WE ABIDE IN CHRIST

Aaron Williams recorded a beautiful spirit-filled song entitled, “Abide”. The chorus goes like this:

You’re the way the truth and the life

You’re the well that never runs dry

I’m the branch and You are the vine

Draw me close and teach me to **abide**

That’s what this chapter is all about. We now understand what it means to **abide in Christ continually** and we know how important it is for a **“more abundant life.”** So, how do we do it? Initially, we must be convinced of the need to pursue this lofty goal and have a strong desire to do so. “Blessed are those who hunger and thirst for righteousness, For they shall **be filled**.” (Matt. 5:6) “And you will seek Me and find Me, when you search for Me with all your heart.” (Jer. 29:13) God wants us to surrender to Him. And surrendering to Him is never just a one-time event. Apostle Paul said, “I die daily.” (1 Cor. 15:31) Here is a list of practical ways from which you can choose to **abide in Him**:

PRAISE GOD: Our days should be full of praise because Jesus is so worthy! **Praise Him throughout your day** in those empty moments. **“From the rising of the sun to its going down The Lord’s name is to be praised.”** (Ps. 113:3) “I WILL **bless the Lord at all times; His praise shall continually be in my mouth**.” (Ps. 34:1)

THANK GOD: "Enter into His gates with thanksgiving, and into His courts with praise." (Ps. 100:4) "**In everything give thanks**; for this is the will of God in Christ Jesus for you." (1 Thess. 5:18) Sarah Young said, "Thank Him even for difficult times because they can demonstrate the perfect match between our neediness and God's desire and ability to meet our needs." The significance of trials can fade while we thank Him and **dwell in His presence**.

TRUST GOD: "Commit your way to the Lord, Trust also in Him, And He shall bring it to pass." (Ps. 37:5) Trusting God full time provides power to **abide in Him** and experience the riches and glory in Christ Jesus. Trusting God is so important that the word trust was used at least fifty-five times in the Book of Psalms. King David frequently confirmed his trust in God by saying, "I trust in You." (Ps. 25:2) We need to do the same. Learn to trust Jesus especially when things go wrong. "Trust in the Lord with all your heart, and lean not unto your own understanding; **In all your ways acknowledge Him**, And He shall direct your paths." (Prov. 3:5-6)

FIX YOUR MIND ON HIM: "**Set your mind on things above**, not on things on the earth." (Col. 3:2) "You will keep him in perfect peace, **Whose mind is stayed on You, Because he trusts in You**." (Ps. 26:3 I heard about a man who made money from dog-fighting events by encouraging people to bet on which one would win. He had two dogs; sometimes one would win, and sometimes the other would win. When asked why that was so, he said, "I starve one and feed the other." We win when we **feed mostly on Christ within us**. Callie Penn, a leader of our Seniors' Group at TRBC, frequently refers to a special prayer of his: **"Help me to keep my mind's attention and my heart's affection focused and centered on You."**

PRAY WITHOUT CEASING: "Rejoice always, **pray without ceasing, in everything give thanks**; for this is the will of God in Christ Jesus for you." (1 Thess. 5:16-18) We should be in **ongoing communications with God** during every hour of every day. We should pray about small things and large things. I encourage you to pray this large prayer based on Second Chronicles 7:14: Oh Lord, I pray that Your people who are called by Your name will humble ourselves, and **pray without ceasing, seek Your face**, and turn from our wicked ways, and that You will hear from Heaven, and will forgive our sin and heal our land. Amen. If you would like to be like Jesus, you should pray without ceasing because that is what He did for us. "Therefore He is also able to save to the uttermost those who come to God through Him, since He **always lives to make intercession for them**." (He. 7:25)

READ OR LISTEN TO GOD'S WORD: God's word plays an inherent role in helping us **remain filled and influenced by the Holy Spirit**. God speaks to us while reading or hearing His word. "For the word of God is living and powerful, and sharper than any two-edged sword, piercing even to the division of soul and spirit, and of joints and marrow, and is a discerner of the thoughts and intents of the heart." (He. 4:12) "All Scripture is given by inspiration of God, and is profitable for doctrine, for reproof, for correction, for instruction in righteousness, that the man of God may be complete, thoroughly equipped for every good work." (2 Tim. 3:16) **"Let the word of Christ dwell in you richly..."** (Col. 3:16) We **remain filled with the Holy Spirit** by seeking Him through His word. Remember, Jesus quoted Scripture to avoid sin.

I recently read an interesting article about one of Billy Graham's grandsons. He was visiting his famous grandfather one day and observed Billy walking from the bedroom to the kitchen. Billy stopped at an open Bible for a couple of seconds to read something. When Billy returned to the bedroom, he stopped again to briefly read something else. Billy's grandson flippantly asked him what good could that possibly do? Billy said, **"I sip on God's word all day long!"**

MEDITATE ON GOD'S WORD: Memorize helpful Bible verses and meditate on them. "This Book of the Law **shall not depart from your mouth, but you shall meditate in it day and night**, that you may observe to do according to all that is written in it. For then you will make your way prosperous, and then you will have good success." (Josh. 1:8) A great time to meditate is before you go to sleep or when you lie awake at night. "**Meditate within your heart on your bed**, and be still." (Ps. 4:4) A similar verse says, "Be still and know that I am God..." (Ps. 46:10) There have been many times while lying awake **aware of God's presence**, but without fixing my thoughts on anything specific, that God gave me helpful ideas to include in this booklet. I would then get up, add another note to my collection, and go back to bed. Praise the Lord!

OBEY GOD'S WORD: "If you keep My commandments, **you will abide in My love**, just as I have kept My Father's commandments and **abide in His love**." (Jn. 15:10) Billy Graham said, **"We will be filled as we yield and obey."** Also, **as we are filled with His Spirit**, power is readily available to help us overcome temptations and the sinful nature. Apostle Paul confirmed this when he said, "I say then: **Walk in the Spirit**, and you shall not fulfill the lust of the flesh." (Gal. 5:16)

CONFESS SINS: Nothing will impede or stop the flow of divine power faster than sin or disobedience in our lives. Of course, God will forgive us when we confess our sins, but we must also forgive those who sin against us as part of the deal. "If we confess our sins, He is faithful and just to forgive us our sins and to cleanse us from all unrighteousness." (1 Jn. 1:9) "And forgive us our debts, As we forgive our debtors." (Mt. 6:12)

CARRY A SONG IN YOUR HEART: A great way to continue your day after a quiet time with God is to pick a favorite praise song and play it over and over again in your heart throughout the day. "Come before His presence with singing." (Ps. 100:2) "And do not be drunk with wine, in which is dissipation; but **be filled with the Spirit, speaking to one another in psalms and hymns and spiritual songs, singing and making melody in your heart to the Lord**." (Eph. 5:18-19) Also, listen to spiritual music when you have a chance.

LOVE GOD, AND LOVE PEOPLE: "And you shall love the Lord your God with all your heart, with all your soul, with all your mind, and with all your strength. This is the first commandment. And the second, like it, is this: You shall love your neighbor as yourself. There is no other commandment greater than these." (Mk. 12:30-31) Herbert Lockyer connected the need for demonstrating love with **abiding in Christ** when he said, "**If men are to know that we are filled with the Spirit, we must be filled with love**. We must reflect His loving nature." Similarly, Andrew Murray said, "Oh, do let us learn the lesson and pray God fervently to teach it to His people, that a church or a Christian professing to have the Holy Spirit must prove it by the exhibition of Christlike love. But what unlovely traits are ours, and how unlovable we are! Unconquered temper, prevailing selfishness, harsh judgments, unkind words, unlovely ways, impatience all alike proclaim the absence of the Spirit's love." "...God is love, and he who abides in love **abides in God**, and God in him." (1 John 4:16) As we **abide in Christ**, His characteristics, such as the fruit of the Spirit, will flow through us. "But the fruit of the Spirit is love, joy, peace, longsuffering, kindness, goodness, faithfulness, gentleness, self-control." (Gal. 5:22-23)

BE ESPECIALLY INTENTIONAL ABOUT ABIDING IN CHRIST WHILE TALKING WITH PEOPLE:
Keep your mind's eyes fixed on Jesus every time you talk with someone because He will help you as to what to say and how to say it with a loving attitude. **"My eyes are ever toward the Lord."** (Ps. 25:15) **"I have set the Lord always before me."** (Ps. 16:8)

BE ESPECIALLY INTENTIONAL ABOUT ABIDING IN CHRIST DURING TRIALS :
And trials will definitely come! "Beloved, do not think it strange concerning the fiery trial which is to try you, as though some strange thing happened to you." (1 Pet. 4:12) As you know, trials can be minor in nature or they can be major challenges. And believe it or not, God's word tells us that we should even glory in our tribulations, but we can do so only if we are **abiding in Him**. "Therefore, having been justified by faith, we have peace with God **through our Lord Jesus Christ, through whom** also we have access by faith into this grace in which we stand, and rejoice in hope of the glory of God. And not only that, but we also **glory in tribulations**, knowing that tribulation produces perseverance; and perseverance, character, and character, hope. Now hope does not disappoint, because the love of God has been poured out in our hearts by the Holy Spirit who was given to us." (Ro. 5: 1-5) So, we need to be prepared for trials and tribulations, and the best way to prepare is to **abide in Christ continually**, **"for without Me, you can do nothing."** (Jn. 15:5)

PERSIST: If you are currently not being **filled with the Spirit** throughout each day and you really want to with all your heart, you must persist with your efforts to discipline your mind as you pursue that goal, even though it may not be easy. "You will seek Me and find Me when you search for Me with all your heart." (Jer. 29:13) "...let us run with endurance the race that is set before us." (He. 12:1) **"I press toward the goal for the prize of the upward call of God in Christ Jesus."** (Phil. 3:14)

Just remember that everything that is now easy for you to do, was once difficult.

IDENTIFY REMINDERS TO ABIDE: It is easy to get distracted from **remaining filled with the Spirit all day long**. Brother Lawrence understood this and explained, "You aren't the only one to be distracted from the **presence of God**; I understand completely. Our minds are so flighty." A good way to remember to abide in Christ is to select a meaningful Scripture verse first thing every morning, and review it mentally as often as you can throughout the day. As you do, you will be abiding in Christ and memorizing Scripture at the same time. Try to always be aware of the time of day, and use it to remind you to fix your thoughts on Jesus. Use the act of walking to remind you to abide. Walking makes me think of Galatians 5:16, which says, "I say then, **walk in the Spirit**, and you shall not fulfill the lust of the flesh." Perhaps an accountability partner may encourage you to keep at it. Develop your own reminders, and enjoy your **walk with Him**!

BENEFITS OF ABIDING IN CHRIST

"Bless the Lord, O my soul; And forget not all His benefits." (Ps. 103:2) There are many benefits of being **filled with the Holy Spirit**, beginning with the **awareness of God's holy presence**. The song, Holy Spirit, begins with, "there's nothing worth more, that will ever come close, no thing can compare, you're our living hope - **Your presence Lord**!" It goes on with, "Your glory God is what our hearts long for, to be overcome by **Your presence Lord**." **Abiding in Christ** is not dependent on your feelings, but feelings can, occasionally, be one of the benefits. Here is a list of many other benefits of **abiding in Christ**:

ANSWERED PRAYERS: "**If you abide in Me, and My words abide in you**, you will ask what you desire, and it shall be done for you." (Jn. 15:7)

AVOIDANCE OF SIN: Please don't ever forget: **"Whoever abides in Him does not sin..."** (1 Jn .3:6) and "I say then: **Walk in the Spirit, and you shall not fulfill the lust of the flesh**." (Gal. 5:16). Also, remember that Jesus demonstrated how to avoid sin by being **filled with the Spirit** and by quoting Scripture. (Luke Chapter 4)

BLESSED: "Blessed is the man who listens to me, **Watching daily at my gates, Waiting at the posts of my doors**." (Prov. 8:34)

MATURE SPIRITUALLY: "But the fruit of the Spirit is love, joy, peace, longsuffering, kindness, goodness, faithfulness, gentleness, self-control. Against such there is no law." (Gal. 5:22-23) As we **remain filled with the Spirit**, His power flows through us changing us to be more like Jesus and empowering us in various ways to achieve His purpose.

DIRECTION FOR LIFE: "Trust in the Lord with all your heart, And lean not on your own understanding; **In all your ways acknowledge Him**, And He shall direct your paths." (Prov. 3:5-6)

FRUITFUL AND ABUNDANT LIVING: "**This Book of the Law shall not depart from your mouth, but you shall meditate in it day and night**, that you may observe to do according to all that is written in it. For then you will make your way prosperous, and then you will have good success." (Josh. 1:8) "I am the vine, you are the branches, He who **abides in Me**, and I in him, bears much fruit; for without Me you can do nothing." (Jn. 15:5) Warren Wiersbe described "**abiding in Christ as maintaining constant fellowship with Him**, allowing His life to work through us for fruit. He emphasized that **abiding** is not a passive state but **a continuous, active relationship**, and it Is **essential for producing good fruit**. The **secret of abiding**, according to Wiersbe, is **obeying**, which in turn stems from loving God."

HELP WITH RELATIONSHIPS: "But if we **walk in the light as He is in the light**, we have fellowship with one another, and the blood of Jesus Christ His Son, cleanses us from all sin." (1 Jn. 1:7) Tim Dilena, Senior Pastor of Times Square Church, said, "Our fellowship with people is contingent on our **walk with God**. In order for there to be fellowship, according to 1 Jn. 1:7, there must be light and blood. The light keeps everything open and accountable; the blood keeps everything forgivable if there is a sin encounter."

JOYFUL LIFE: "...**In Your presence** is fullness of joy." (Ps. 16:11) "You have made me exceedingly glad **with your presence**." (Ps 21:6)

PEACE: "You will keep him in perfect peace, **Whose mind is stayed on You**, Because he trusts in you." (Isa. 26:3)

STRENGTH TO DO GOD'S WILL: "But **those who wait on the Lord** Shall renew their strength; They shall mount up with wings like eagles, They shall run and not be weary, They shall walk and not faint." (Isa. 40:31) "I can do all things **through Christ** who strengthens me." (Phil. 4:13) Billy Graham said, "I believe God gives us the strength of the Holy Spirit commensurate with the tasks He gives us. When God calls us to any task He also supplies the power for that task." One of the names of Jesus is Emmanuel, which means "God with us." He is all-present, all-knowing, and all-powerful. "Jesus Christ is the same yesterday and today and forever." (He. 13:8) With immediate and ongoing access to His perfect knowledge, influence, and power, we can accomplish anything in His will.

BOLDNESS FOR WITNESSING: "..They were all **filled with the Holy Spirit, and they spoke the word of God with boldness**." (Acts 4:31) "But you shall receive power when the Holy Spirit has come upon you; and you shall be witnesses to Me in Jerusalem, and in all Judea and Samaria, and to the end of the earth." (Acts 1:8) Unfortunately, according to the Barna Group, a Christian research organization, a very small percentage of Christians have ever presented the Gospel to a non-Christian! Many Christians believe that only preachers, teachers, and evangelists need to share the Gospel with others. However, the Bible makes it very clear, in many verses, that God wants every Christian to explain the Gospel to non-Christians. Acts 8:1-4 is a great example, explaining that 100% of the early Christians from Jerusalem preached the Gospel because they were **filled with the Holy Spirit**. Most Christians don't witness because of either fear planted by Satan or lack of interest and concern. **The passion and boldness for witnessing comes as we constantly abide in Christ and are filled with the Spirit**, "for without Me, you can do nothing." (Jn: 15:5) D.L. Moody "emphasized that those who **abide in Christ** are motivated to share the Gospel and lead others to Him, demonstrating a life of service and compassion."

WISDOM: "Therefore, brethren, seek out from among you seven men of good reputation, **full of the Holy Spirit and wisdom**, whom we may appoint over this business." (Acts 6:3)

PROTECTION: Many years ago, I was on a business trip in Ankara, Turkey, where I stayed in a room on an upper floor in a very tall hotel. When I first arrived, I was captivated by the beautiful view, so I stepped out on the balcony for a better look. The railing was near the door, unusually low, and the step down to the balcony floor was lower than I expected. So, when I stepped down with my eyes glued to the view, I fell forward and almost went over the low railing! My experience was very frightening, with heart-pounding emotions. With tears in my eyes, I thanked the dear Lord for saving me from certain death! During the mornings leading up to my trip, I had been reading through the Book of Psalms. The next morning, after the incident, my regularly scheduled reading began with Psalm 91. This scripture jumped from the page, and my heart began pounding all over again: "Because you have made the Lord, who is **my refuge**, Even the Most High, **your dwelling place**, No evil shall befall you, Nor shall any plague come near your dwelling; for He shall give His angels charge over you, To keep you in all your ways.In their hands they shall bear you up, Lest you dash your foot against a stone." (Ps. 91:9-12)

As born-again believers, we will experience some or all of the above benefits and even more depending on how little or how much time we spend **abiding in Christ** and how well we follow His commands, because God's word uses the term "if" as a condition for many of these benefits. Here are a few examples from Scripture: "If you **abide in Me**, and My words abide in you." (Jn. 15:7) "If you keep my commandments". (Jn. 15:10); and "If My people who are called by My name will humble themselves, and pray and **seek My face**..." (2 Chr. 7:14) "God's word in Psalms 105:4 commands us to, **"Seek His face evermore"**. We really need to **seek His face** all the time and especially for "such a time as this."

I believe, generally speaking, the more **time we spend with God** and the more consistently we follow His commands, the more we will enjoy the benefits, but there is no magic formula. God alone, in His infinite wisdom and grace, determines the timing and nature of keeping His promises. Also, the more we **dwell with Him**, the more we will mature spiritually, the more we will meaningfully impact God's Kingdom, and the more we will glorify Him. There will be tests and trials, of course, but we must keep trusting and obeying no matter what. We cannot out-give God by our efforts to **abide in Him**.

My prayer is that this booklet will not be just another book that you will read and then toss aside for the next book. Instead, I pray that, because of the amazing life-changing results and eternal impact that can be achieved by **abiding in Him**, it will be a source of training material that you will persist to study and apply until you remain **filled with the Holy Spirit**.

CONCLUSION

A key element in God's design, for His delight and for the benefit of mankind, is our potential to **abide in Him** both here on earth and throughout eternity. The book of Psalms addresses this clearly: "Lord, You have been our **dwelling place** in all generations;" (Ps. 90:1) and "...**I will dwell in the house of the Lord Forever**." (Ps. 23:6)

To fulfill this potential, Christians must discipline themselves to **abide in Christ continually - practicing His presence**, because all else depends on it! So, what is the "all else" that depends on it? It is everything meaningful in life and everything of eternal significance. It is the influence and power of the Holy Spirit. It is a high-quality relationship with God and with others. It is answered prayers. It is help to overcome temptations, bad habits and sin in our lives. It is help to develop godliness and Christ-like characteristics like "love, joy, peace, longsuffering, kindness, goodness, faithfulness, gentleness, self-control." (Gal. 5:22-23) It is boldness for sharing Christ. It is spiritual fruit, met needs, and abundant living. It is wisdom, guidance, divine protection, and strength to do His will. It is "exceedingly abundantly above all that we ask or think, according to the power that works in us." (Eph. 3:20)

I thank God so much for His amazing gift of the Holy Spirit and for His help to **keep us filled and empowered**, as Apostle Paul revealed 2000 years ago. I also thank Him that the early Christians **practiced His**

presence in their daily lives as they spread the Gospel of Jesus Christ around the world. As for me, "One thing I have desired of the Lord, That will I seek: That I may **dwell in the house of the Lord All the days of my life**, To behold the beauty of the Lord, And to inquire in His temple." (Ps. 27:4)

"And now, little children, **abide in Him, that when He appears, we may have confidence and not be ashamed before Him at His coming**." (1 Jn. 2:28) I pray, after the Apostle Paul, "that He would grant you, according to the riches of His glory, to be strengthened with might **through His Spirit** in the inner man, that Christ may dwell in your hearts through faith; that you, being rooted and grounded in love, may be able to comprehend with all the saints what is the width and length and depth and height - to know the love of Christ which passes knowledge; that **you may be filled with all the fullness of God**." (Eph. 3:16-19)

The last precious recorded words that Jesus said before ascending into heaven were: "All authority has been given to Me in heaven and on earth. Go therefore and make disciples of all the nations, baptizing them in the name of the Father and of the Son and of the Holy Spirit, teaching them to observe all things that I have commanded you; and lo, I am with you always, even to the end of the age." (Matt. 28:18-20). Jesus commanded every Christian to lead people to Christ, encourage them to be baptized, and teach them how to mature as disciples so they can do likewise. Jesus also mentioned that He would be with us, which enables us to abide in Him and follow His commands. That was His wonderful plan for us as He made His departure. God's main purpose for us is to glorify Him by abiding in Christ and fulfilling the Great Commission, which will help expand His Kingdom.

Now, if you are a born-again believer, have read this booklet and committed to abide in Christ, engaging the power of the Holy Spirit, who will "...teach you all things, and bring to your remembrance all things that I said to you." (John 14:26), you are fully equipped to fulfill the Great Commission! He will also provide you power and wisdom to do what He wants you to do and be who He wants you to be. So, I pray that you will use this free non-threatening and effective digital booklet, containing the gospel and detailed information on abiding in Christ, to help many others enjoy that "more abundant life" that Jesus came to give us. And I pray, as other readers learn to abide in Christ, the Holy Spirit will be their ultimate teacher, who will help them also fulfill the Great Commission. You can simply attach a digital copy of this booklet to an email, refer them to thirdgreatestcommandment.org, or give them a hard copy and say something like: "Here is a little booklet that I found to be very interesting and helpful. I hope you take a little time to read it, let me know what you think, and then pass it on to others". It's now time to begin or continue a Spirit-filled journey that will revive your life and the lives of many others! May you be richly blessed as you obey God's command to abide in Christ all the time and fulfill HIs Great Commission!!

Note: Now, please go to You Tube and request the song "Abide", by Aaron Williams.

ANNEX

MORE WAYS OF ABIDING IN CHRIST

- Daily quiet time with God, reading the Bible, praying and meditating.
- Regular worship at a good Bible-honoring church.
- Small group participation with like-minded Christians for Bible study and fellowship.
- Service to God and others using your spiritual gift(s).
- Sharing your faith verbally with non-Christians.
- Giving to God through church and to people in need.

Made in the USA
Coppell, TX
24 June 2026

83185225R00031